CATS CATS CATS

OTHER BOOKS BY S. GROSS

How Gross

I Am Blind and My Dog Is Dead

An Elephant Is Soft and Mushy

More Gross

Why Are Your Papers in Order?

Dogs Dogs Dogs

CATS CATS CATS

a collection of great cat cartoons

EDITED BY S. GROSS

PERENNIAL LIBRARY

Harper & Row, Publishers, New York
Cambridge, Philadelphia, San Francisco, Washington
London, Mexico City, São Paulo, Singapore, Sydney

Some of the cartoons in this collection have appeared in the following periodicals and are reprinted by permission of the authors: *Audubon, Better Homes and Gardens, Boys' Life, Campus Life, Cavalier, Cosmopolitan, Diversion, Family Circle, Good Housekeeping, Gourmet, House & Garden, Ladies' Home Journal, National Enquirer, National Lampoon, 1000 Jokes, Oui, Parade, Penthouse, Philadelphia Inquirer Magazine, Playboy, Punch, Saturday Evening Post, Saturday Review, This Week, TV Guide, Vision, Woman's Day, The Yacht.*

Grateful acknowledgment is made for permission to reprint:

Cartoon by George Booth on page 161 from *Playboy.* Copyright © 1974 by Playboy. Reproduced by special permission of *Playboy* magazine.

Cartoons by Roz Chast from *Parallel Universes.* Copyright © 1984 by Roz Chast. Reproduced by permission of the author.

Cartoon by Samuel H. Gross on page 182 reprinted with permission from *TV Guide* magazine. Copyright © 1976 by Triangle Publications, Inc., Radnor, Pennsylvania.

Cartoons by Sidney Harris on pages 164 and 235 from *Playboy.* Copyright © 1971, 1979 by Playboy. Reproduced by special permission of *Playboy* magazine.

Cartoons by Henry Martin on pages 219 and 98 from *Punch.* Copyright © 1979, 1983 by Punch. Reprinted by permission of Rothco Cartoons Inc. and the author.

Cartoons by John S. P. Walker. Reprinted from *Bad Dogs* by John S. P. Walker. Copyright © 1982 by John S. P. Walker. Reprinted by permission of Alfred A. Knopf, Inc. and Methuen and Company, Ltd.

Cartoons by Gahan Wilson on page 78 from *Playboy.* Copyright © 1972 by Playboy. Reproduced by special permission of *Playboy* magazine.

Cartoons copyrighted by *The New Yorker* are indicated throughout the book.

First PERENNIAL LIBRARY edition published 1987.

Designer: Kim Llewellyn

Library of Congress Cataloging-in-Publication Data

Cats cats cats.

1. Cats—Caricatures and cartoons.   2. American wit and humor, Pictorial.   I. Gross, S. (Sam)
NC1426.C28   1989   741.5′973   86-45111
ISBN 0-06-015630-9   89 90 HOR 10 9 8 7 6
ISBN 0-06-096185-6 (pbk)   89 90 HOR 10 9 8 7 6 5 4

"I guess she's the theme again this evening."

ED FRASCINO

LIZA DONNELLY

"There's a silly sign if
I ever saw one."

SAM GROSS

"Brace yourself, Grace. The doctor has discovered
the nature of my allergy."

WILLIAM HOEST

SIDNEY HARRIS

5

"Her landlord kicked her cat!
How did this thing ever get out of Small Claims Court?"

EVERETT OPIE

© 1967 The New Yorker Magazine, Inc.

"Now, don't start complaining till you taste it."

REX MAY (BALOO)

THE CRAZY HOUR

Face gets wild.

Back hunches up. ("Halloween kitty")

Noisy runs after invisible things.

GALUMPH GALUMPH

Back to normal.

ROZ CHAST

9

TIM HAGGERTY

"Could you show me something just a little more scratch-resistant?"

O'NEILL CATHARINE O'NEILL

"Hmm . . . looks like the bottom's falling out of the cat book market!"

"Does that include cats?"

"Now we've only two more kittens to unload."

"She has your eyes."

BERNARD SCHOENBAUM

"We have an important visitor today: the King of the Cats."

ED FISHER

CATHERINE SIRACUSA

"I hope you don't mind cat hairs."

FELIPE GALINDO (FEGGO)

20

"I think we'll take it, subject to his approval."

ED FRASCINO

21

"Have you been made to feel welcome?"

MORT GERBERG

23

"Don't forget to give
Gertrude her pill."

DON OREHEK

24

Q: WHAT KIND of CATS ARE MOST FRIENDLY?

A: THOSE WHO HAVE THE WORST BREATH.

REVILO

OLIVER CHRISTIANSON (REVILO)

25

BERNARD SCHOENBAUM

"Peasant!"

HENRY MARTIN

"Our only consolation is that in about eleven years the controlling stockholder will be dead."

1. _____

2. _____

3. _____

AARON BACALL   A. BACALL

"You're purring. I like that in a cat."

JOHN CALLAHAN

S.GROSS

SAM GROSS

VAHAN SHIRVANIAN

"This is a solo number, if you don't mind."

31

LEE LORENZ

"We've been living together for six years, toots. How about getting hitched?"

ORLANDO BUSINO

"Did you get a description of the cat?"

THE VIGIL

1

2

3

4

5

6

7

8

35

(continued)

9

10

11

12

ED FRASCINO

"I like dogs better. Dogs kiss."

37

P.C. VEY

"Have you ever read the label on a can of cat food? It reads 'all beef and beef byproducts.' . . .
Now tell me, do we look like either beef or beef byproducts?"

"You might as well introduce him to the 'treats' you got last year."

39

"I *do* apologize, Rinehart. The cat has never bitten anyone previously."

"The Graysons are on vacation in Europe. I'm the sitter."

"It's 20 cents a pound cheaper. *That's* why!"

"The artist was one of the first to experiment with the use of velvet
as an alternative to canvas."

BILL WOODMAN

45

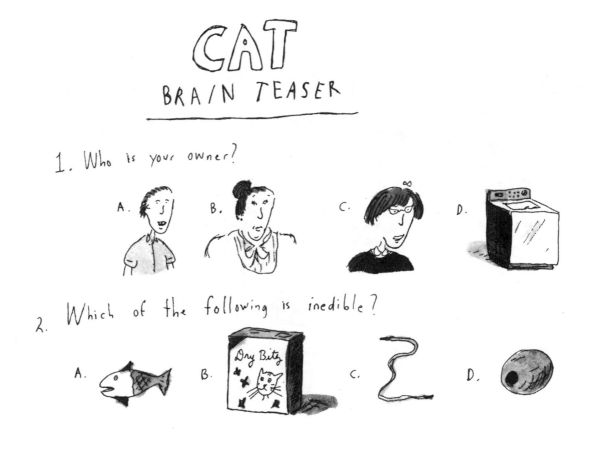

3. Name the scratchpost.

A.

B.

C.

D.

4. What happened to your little mouse-toy?

A.

Under couch

B.

Behind bookcase

C.

Turned into a ghost

D.

I don't know and
what's the difference?

R. Chast

"Actually it's turned out to be more of a cat feeder."

WILLIAM HOEST

"... and that's why a cat on a boat is considered bad luck."

BILL MAUL

48

"He's a confirmed bachelor."

ED FRASCINO

49

"No more Kitty-bits, Jenny. We're all Seventh Day Adventists now."

CATHARINE O'NEILL

"What's there to discuss?"

MICHAEL MASLIN

51

"Who do you think you're staring at!"

DON OREHEK

"Honey, I think the cat wants out!"

JOHN CALLAHAN

WALTER GALLUP

"He's never been sick a day in his life except for an occasional fur ball."

"*Now* you tell me you get airsick!"

S.GROSS

SAM GROSS

FELIPE GALINDO (FEGGO)

"He's merely putting the cat out, but he makes
such a drama out of doing it."

Noel Watson

ALEX NOEL WATSON

58

OLIVER CHRISTIANSON (REVILO)

"Did you know you could throw out your back doing that?"

TIM HAGGERTY

ANTHONY TABER

JO LINKERT

"Good news, Mr. Smith! The cat
got down safely."

"Meow! Pass it on!"

BORIS DRUCKER

BOOTH

GEORGE BOOTH

"He sure fooled me . . . . I didn't think he gave a damn about anything."

THOMAS CHENEY

63

ED FRASCINO

"When you told me you were an ailurophile I thought you were into some kind of kinky sex."

"Jonathan!"

DON OREHEK

65

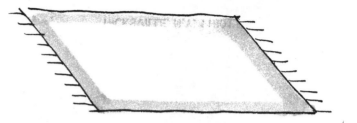

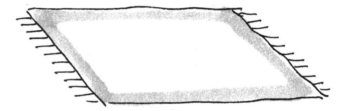

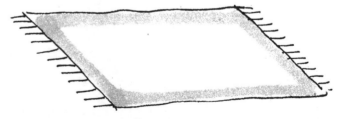

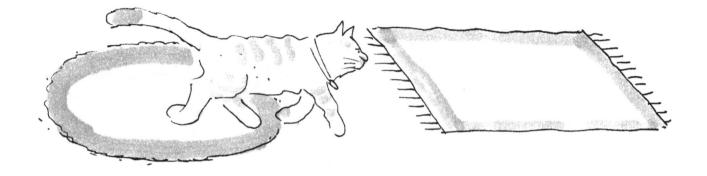

BERNARD SCHOENBAUM

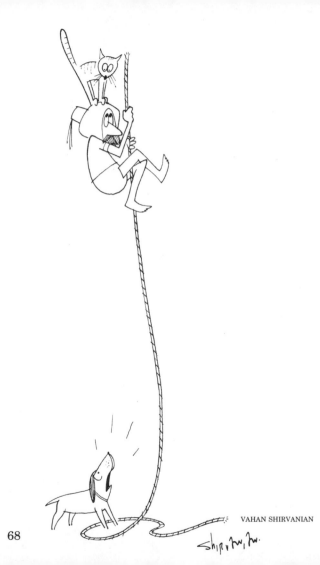

VAHAN SHIRVANIAN

HENRY MARTIN

"I wrote a letter to the president of the company about the red food dye in your Turkey and Chicken Parts and he wrote back a two-page letter, the bottom line of which was something about consumerism, test marketing, and finicky eaters."

MORT GERBERG

"You wouldn't be purring so smugly if you knew we were careening into poverty."

69

"Look, I already have a cat clock, a cat calendar, cat cushions, and a cat lamp—so beat it."

MICHAEL MASLIN

THE PUSSYCAT OLYMPICS

MICK STEVENS

71

SAM GROSS

"What is it with you, anyway?"

FRANK MODELL

"According to the note, they voted 8 to 3
to come live with their father."

BILL MAUL

73

"Sit up!"

"Lie down!"

"Heel!"

"Give a paw!"

"Roll over!"

CATHARINE O'NEILL

"Congratulations, Mr. Stevens. Sally graduates
summa cum laude from the Canby Cat
Obedience School."

"I know it's not Perrier, but that's all that's available."

"Darn! We forgot the non-temperamental cats!"

MICHAEL CRAWFORD

"Cat out?"

GAHAN WILSON

"Here, puss, puss, puss!"

FELIPE GALINDO (FEGGO)

ARNIE LEVIN
© 1975 The New Yorker Magazine, Inc.

"I haven't been happy, but I pretend for her sake."

ED FRASCINO

VAHAN SHIRVANIAN

"Two martinis, very dry, one with an olive, one with a goldfish."

TIM HAGGERTY

BERNARD SCHOENBAUM

83

"City mouse, country mouse—
I'm not particular."

CHARLES SAUERS

ORLANDO BUSINO

"First the good news—kitty finally came home. . . ."

84

"Bank robbery, safe cracking, counterfeiting, forgery, no, no, no . . . you had to become a cat burglar!"

THOMAS CHENEY

ALLEY CAT

STUART LEEDS

"Pegler drank a toast to Mrs. Pegler, then he drank a toast to each of Mrs. Pegler's thirteen cats. That's too damn many cats!"

GEORGE BOOTH

THE FOUR CAT BREEDS

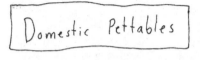

These cats can take as much affection as you're willing to dish out. This includes hugging by 2-year-olds. They can be found anywhere and everywhere. Look for the tell-tale "I aim to please" expression and congenital bow.

These felines are rarely seen except under furniture and in the back of closets. You might have one and not even know it.

$ 6,000.²⁹

True Costabundles are recognized by their subliminal pricetags and nitwit owners. They tend to do a lot of sleeping

Stranges

This unfortunate group appears mainly in cat shows and in the imaginations of people who think of themselves as "cat fanciers." Hairlessness, wrinkly skin, rat-tails, and weird facial expressions are a few of their attributes.

R. Chast
ROZ CHAST

JOHN CASSADY

"Just because he's been declawed—
don't think he's any less dangerous."

AARON BACALL

"She can't understand it. You're not shedding and she is."

ORLIN

RICHARD ORLIN

91

"I'll tell you one thing, Percy, there aren't many cats like you."

"Edgar, please run down to the shopping center right away, and get some milk and cat food. Don't get canned tuna, or chicken, or liver, or any of those awful combinations. Shop around and get a surprise. The pussies like surprises."

93

HOURS OF FUN

MICK STEVENS

94

"You're getting fat, Jason, too fat to do anything."

BORIS DRUCKER

"Of course she's beautiful. She sleeps eighteen hours a day."

ED FRASCINO

BERNARD SCHOENBAUM

"That's nothing. You should have been here five minutes ago when the dish ran away with the spoon."

HENRY MARTIN

"I tell you, the book has everything—sex, history, conscious-
ness, and cats!"

WILLIAM HAMILTON
© 1977 The New Yorker Magazine, Inc.

COMPLAINTS

S. GROSS
SAM GROSS

1

2

3

4

5

6

VAHAN SHIRVANIAN

100

"Well, I hope you're proud of yourself!"

"We have fourteen cats, but Kevin thinks we only have twelve."

"Boots is getting too fat to sleep on the car!"

DON OREHEK

"There, it's down! Now give her nine of these pills daily."

ORLANDO BUSINO

"Cats are *so* independent!"

"Pounce!"

CHARLES SAUERS

"Your cat is entering my sphere of influence!"

BORIS DRUCKER

THE
Evolution
of
Catfish

John S.P. Walker

JOHN S.P. WALKER

"I think he realizes what a lucky kitty he is."

ED FRASCINO

OLIVER CHRISTIANSON (REVILO)

111

"I used to have lots of little pussycats, but I decided it was easier
to have one great big pussycat."

LEE LORENZ

112

113

"He really needs a bath but the tab on his
collar says to dry clean only."

ANDY WYATT

AARON BACALL

"That's a sacrilege!"

"We found her hiding in one of the closets."

115

1

2

3

4

BERNARD SCHOENBAUM

JERRY MARCUS

"It seems the only thing you remembered to do around here was to put the cat out!"

117

"Yes, my darling—I *know* that Chessy is crying out for you—and so am *I!*"

MORT GERBERG

"You're going to have a nice long life and have lots of kittens. Now scat!"

ARNOLDO FRANCHIONI

"They're Siamese cats."

CHONG

TENG

J.J. SEMPÉ

"I didn't mind it so much before Flossy had kittens."

122

JOHN JONIK

MICHAEL MASLIN

Something the Cat Dragged In

"It's not that I don't trust you, Estelle, but before I eat this oatmeal
I want to see the box that it came in."

BUD GRACE

"My! Aren't we bright-eyed and bushy-tailed this morning."

BERNARD SCHOENBAUM

125

"At first it was the occasional bit of tunafish and, I don't know, one thing just led to another."

CALLAHAN

127

"Cats—you can't live with them, and you can't live without them."

128

"So tell us—what is all this controversy *really* about?"

"Aw quit your bellyaching, you're the one who got drunk and brought the damn thing home."

BILL WOODMAN

130

JACK ZIEGLER

"I liked it, but I still don't like the real ones."

VAHAN
SHIRVANIAN

"Are you coming down or am I coming
up there?"

131

The Allergic Guest

MICK STEVENS

"Everyone be home by two o'clock!"

BOOTH

GEORGE BOOTH
© 1985 The New Yorker Magazine, Inc.

"Are you still feeding that alley cat?"

ORLANDO BUSINO

135

BERNARD SCHOENBAUM

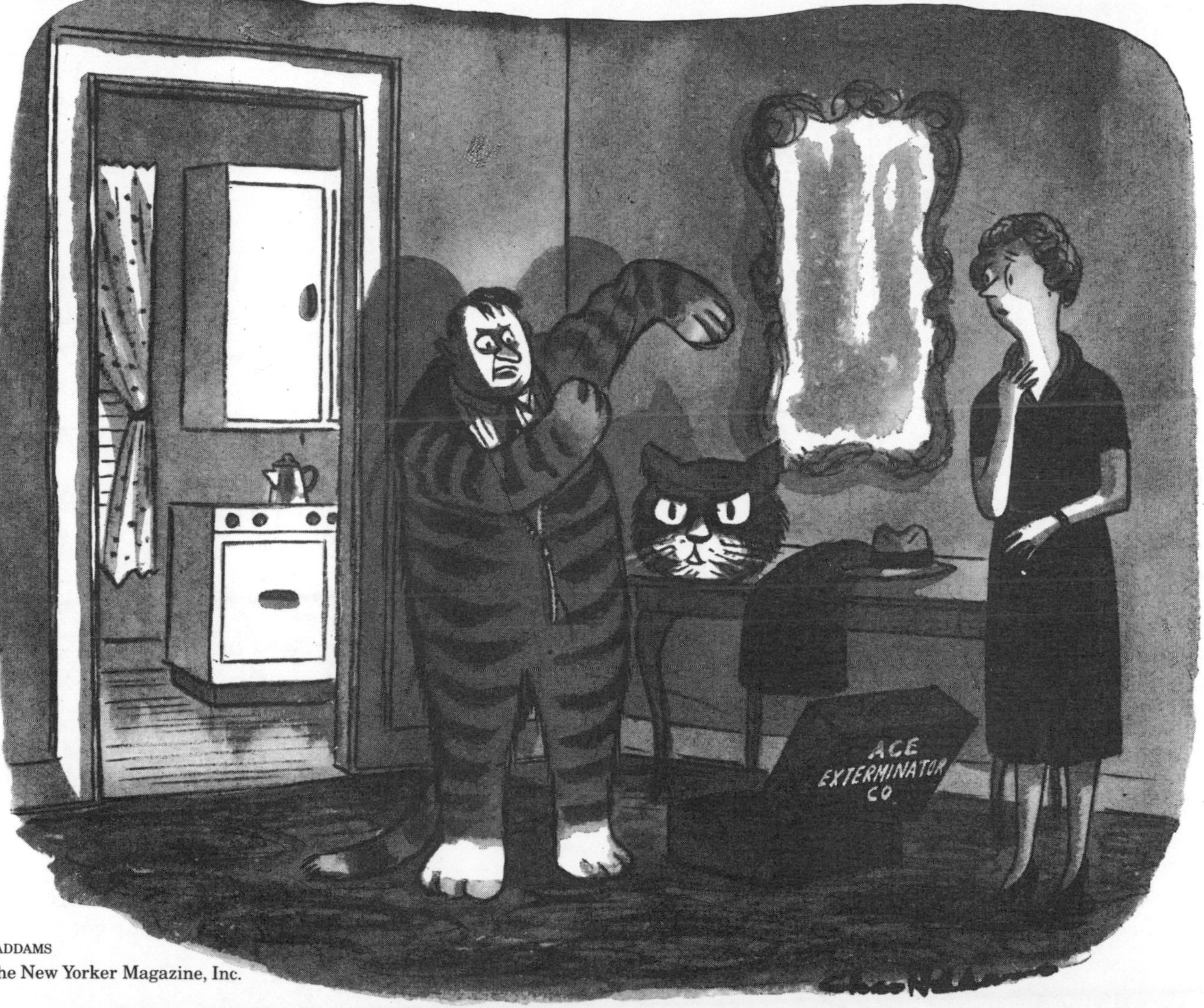

CHARLES ADDAMS

ED FRASCINO

"Has one of you been nosing around
among my souvenirs again?"

BORIS DRUCKER

"Hi there, this is a cat food commercial. I'll wait
while you get your cat."

BILL WOODMAN

HENRY MARTIN

"You may go out, but no concertizing."

ORLANDO BUSINO

"Her flea collar is too tight because
you haven't changed it since she was
a kitten."

"The fact that you cats were considered sacred
in ancient Egypt cuts no ice with me."

J.B. HANDELSMAN

JACK ZIEGLER

DON OREHEK

"How was your day at the fish market, dear?"

"You know what you need? You need
a backpack."

JARED LEE

ED FISHER

"What I really can't stand is his 'more
familiar than thou' attitude."

143

MICHAEL MASLIN

BILL MAUL

"Putty took a wife. Her name was Pussums, and she bore him Little Gentleman, Biddy Boo, Savor Tooth, Fluffy, Harry Cat, and Caesar. Then Little Gentleman begat Little Gentleman II and Friday and Twinkle Toes and Possum Tail and . . ."

BOOTH

GEORGE BOOTH

"Would it kill you to try a little tenderness?"

ED FRASCINO

MORT GERBERG

148

"What's the matter, dear? . . . cat got your tongue?"

150

CHICKEN·ALERT

"I'll have what she's having."

TIM HAGGERTY

151

HENRY MARTIN

"Concerning my fancyleaf caladium,
you have the right to remain silent
and anything you say may be held
against you."

THOMAS CHENEY *Cheney*

V. GENE MYERS

"No wonder her tongue doesn't feel like sandpaper. It's coated with mouse fur."

AL ROSS

S. GROSS

SAM GROSS

"When she was little, we had a very close relationship,
but now we're just friends."

"It's ten o'clock. Do you know where
your cat is?"

VAHAN SHIRVANIAN

WOODMAN

BILL WOODMAN

JO LINKERT

"I'll see you to the door, Marsha . . . I want
to be sure my cat doesn't slip out."

WILLIAM HOEST

"I realize you're lonely now that the
children are gone, Helen, but . . ."

BERNARD SCHOENBAUM

"Where in the world have you been for the past three months?"

159

GUM for CATS

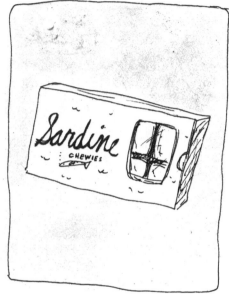

R. Chast

"Let's take the Andantino in C again . . . this time without the cat!"

"Am I talking to *myself?*"

"My advice is keep away from it. You start with catnip, and before you know it, you're on heroin."

SIDNEY HARRIS

"I don't know. Maybe she picked it up from watching figure skaters on the TV."

TIM HAGGERTY

"I'm sorry. I should have warned you. We have bad cat karma."

MORT GERBERG

JOHN JONIK

HENRY MARTIN

". . . and I don't want to find this place in a
shambles when we get back."

167

"All right, come out and we'll talk about it."

"It would appear we're in someone's litterbox."

BILL MAUL

"She bumps into things."

JOHN NORMENT

VAHAN SHIRVANIAN

171

"You're getting him fixed? I didn't know he was broken."

DON OREHEK

PUSS 'N CLOGS

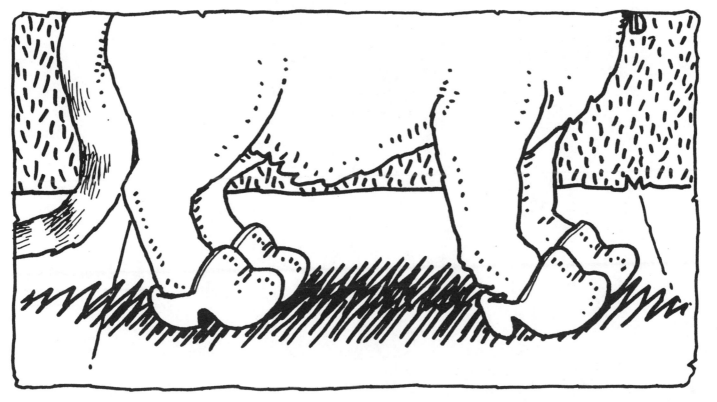

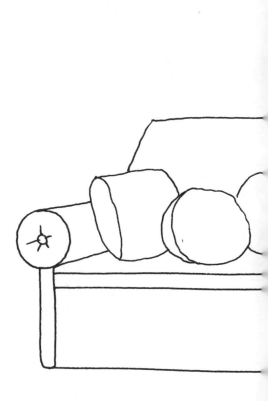

ARNIE LEVIN

174   "You may have nine lives but remember they're concurrent."

CHENEY

THOMAS CHENEY

JACK ZIEGLER

"It's worked out well, actually. They're cat people and I'm, as it turns out, a people cat."

175

JOSEPH FARRIS

ORLANDO BUSINO

"Grace and I have always considered you a friend, Delbert . . . a real friend . . . I mean a *real* friend. . . ."

BILL WOODMAN WOODMAN

"Then as the coup de grâce she turned my own cat against me."

ED FRASCINO

179

"Thank goodness, you remembered the cat food!"

JOHN S.P. WALKER

Man Caught in the Act of Cat-Hurling

SIDNEY HARRIS

"They get along beautifully. The dog thinks he's
a cat and the cat thinks she's a dog."

"Nothing to worry about, folks, I'm just going
to let the cat in."

DON OREHEK

S.GROSS

SAM GROSS

"I'm going to give away all the cats and cancel my magazine subscriptions, and then I'm going to paint ten pickets a day!"

"She used to purr more often before she got spayed."

"I may not know anything about art, but I do know what I hate."

CATHERINE SIRACUSA

PAUL and WILLIE'S SHOE STORE, BEING ATTACKED BY CATS.

BILL WOODMAN

VAHAN SHIRVANIAN

187

ARNIE LEVIN
© 1982 The New Yorker Magazine, Inc.

1

2

3

4

5

6

7

ARNOLDO FRANCHIONI

191

TOO CUTE FOR COMFORT

ROZ CHAST
© 1980 The New Yorker Magazine, Inc.

MICK STEVENS

The Last Robin of Spring

"I'm letting her have one last fling. She's getting declawed tomorrow."

BERNARD SCHOENBAUM

193

"Have you been filling his head with lies about me again?"

ED FRASCINO

AARON BACALL

"Turn around and look cute and adorable!"

JOHN CASSADY

"This year I'm giving all those I care
for dead birds."

HENRY MARTIN

"Muffy, where are you?"

SIDNEY HARRIS

"My favorite is the Late Show. By that time
the set is nice and warm."

O'NEILL
CATHARINE O'NEILL

"You've waited twenty-eight years to tell me,
Marcia? You're a dog person?!"

197

GENE MYERS

TACKY CAT HAVING A RELIGIOUS EXPERIENCE

...IN A NEW OIL SPOT ON THE DRIVEWAY.

REVILO

OLIVER CHRISTIANSON (REVILO)

BERNARD SCHOENBAUM

"Edgar, the cat wants in. And I want *out*."

MORT GERBERG

"Oh, no you don't, Mrs. Grumfeld! You don't get rid of them *that* easily!"

"You have to admit that the kitty was adorable, even
if you can't stand cat-food commercials."

FRANK MODELL
© 1976 The New Yorker Magazine, Inc.

S.GROSS

SAM GROSS

"She *looks* innocent enough, but she's had twenty-nine kids."

"Actually it's quite reasonable when you consider you're buying nine lives."

DON OREHEK

207

MOVIES FOR CATS

Fluffy Gets Fed

Yarn

Of Mice and Birds

R. Chast

"He looks so wistful, let's get him a companion."

DAVID SIPRESS SIPRESS

AL ROSS

GAHAN WILSON
© 1985 The New Yorker Magazine, Inc.

"Just what do you think *you're* up to?"

"Kitty's upset."

210

BERNARD SCHOENBAUM

"Eat it or you won't get any dessert."

VAHAN SHIRVANIAN

"A cat that fetches things. How about *that*? A cat that fetches. I'll be damned."

WARREN MILLER

TIM HAGGERTY

Drucker

BORIS DRUCKER

"Does he have to keep rubbing his whiskers on the floor?"

215

"Sure I know their names. . . . She's
Pretty Kitty and he's Damn Cat."

ANDY WYATT

LEO CULLUM

"I've always felt cats were sort of sneaky—"

An Inside Job

"I have something in common with Queen Elizabeth. We both have animal hair on the furniture. Hers is corgi; mine is cat."

GEORGE BOOTH

HENRY MARTIN

"You know what I like about you? You
don't talk, talk, talk, talk, talk, talk, talk."

ED FRASCINO

"She has hiccups. Can you sneak up and
scare her?"

"I told you not to call him 'pussycat'!"

DON OREHEK

"Cat Yummies *again?*"

JACK ZIEGLER

© 1985 The New Yorker Magazine, Inc.

J.J. SEMPE

© 1985 The New Yorker Magazine, Inc.

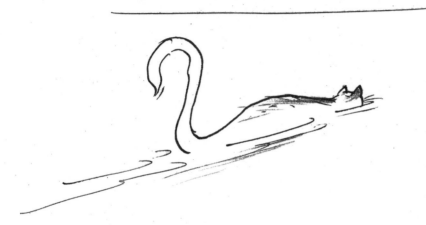

WORDMAN

BILL WOODMAN

FELIPE GALINDO (FEGGO)

"You're a good listener, Ralph."

ED FRASCINO

Cheshire Cat Revisited

"Bye-bye, have a mice day."

MICHAEL MASLIN

225

"I tried to make it from the windowsill to the top of the refrigerator. How about you?"

TONY ROSA

"Today has been difficult, Lucille. Wellington foozled his drive at the ninth tee, and the people next door adopted a new pale-fawn Siamese cat."

227

"Would you let the cat out again, Frank?"

"Did you tell the cat he could have some of these licorice strings?"

BILL MAUL

CAT'S PAJAMAS

ROZ CHAST R. Chast

BOOTH

GEORGE BOOTH

"Boss? I've sprung a leak."

Busino

ORLANDO BUSINO

"Andy and I split. He came home one day with *two* Irish wolfhounds."

P.C.Vey

P.C. VEY

VAHAN SHIRVANIAN

BERNARD SCHOENBAUM

"Alphonse. You're a bum!"

"If you don't have a beeper, then you're sitting on my cat."

SIDNEY HARRIS

237

"We can't afford her full time. We share her with the people across the hall."

ED FRASCINO

"See? Thunder and lightning is God's
way of saying, 'Buffy Barnes, don't
be such a picky eater!' . . ."

BILL MAUL

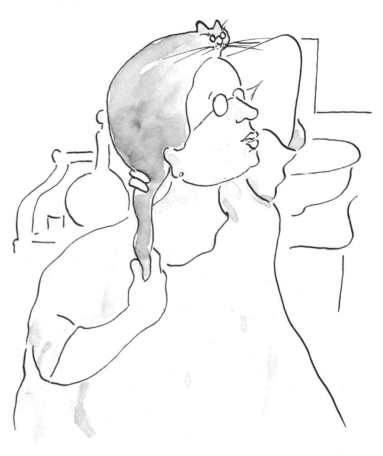

MICHAEL CRAWFORD

After Mary Cassatt: Girl Arranging Her Cat

HENRY MARTIN

"We'll miss you, but I can't promise we won't talk about you when you're gone."

S.GROSS

"I am still trying to figure you out!"   SAM GROSS

BERNARD SCHOENBAUM

"Lord, what a day! On top of everything else, the cat passed away."

Sauers

CHARLES SAUERS

"Gato!"

"Careful. She has an unpredictable
sense of humor."

ED FRASCINO

CAT AEROBICS

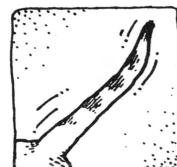

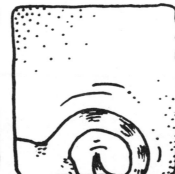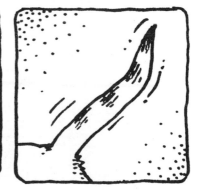

SREVILO

OLIVER CHRISTIANSON (REVILO)

"Meow!"   "Meow!"   "Meow, godammit!"

BORIS DRUCKER

MIXED BREED

CALICO

MALTESE

MANX

ANGORA

PERSIAN

SIAMESE

STUART LEEDS

"Hey Dummy! Who gave you that bell?"

PCVEY

P.C. VEY

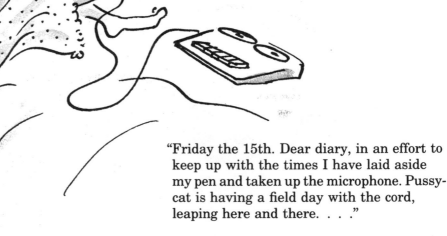

"Friday the 15th. Dear diary, in an effort to keep up with the times I have laid aside my pen and taken up the microphone. Pussy-cat is having a field day with the cord, leaping here and there. . . ."

HENRY MARTIN

246

"I'll bet it's been years since a crumb fell all the way to the floor."

THOMAS CHENEY

JOHN CALLAHAN

"Darling, I told you male cats have a
tendency to spray."

"Now do you believe me that your hair tonic smells like tunafish?"

PETER PORGES

"Must you wear your campaign ribbons in here?"

ED FRASCINO

ORLANDO BUSINO

251

FELIPE GALINDO (FEGGO)